THE PORTAGE POETRY
SERIES

Series Titles

Do Not Feed the Animal
Hikari Leilani Miya

Listening to Mars
Sally Ashton

Glitter City
Bonnie Jill Emanuel

The Trouble with Being a Childless Only Child
Michelle Meyer

Happy Everything
Caitlin Cowan

Dear Lo
Brady Bove

Sadness of the Apex Predator
Dion O'Reilly

The Watching Sky
Judy Brackett Crowe

Let It Be Told in a Single Breath
Russell Thorburn

The Blue Divide
Linda Nemec Foster

Lake, River, Mountain
Mark B. Hamilton

Talking Diamonds
Linda Nemec Foster

Poetic People Power
Tara Bracco (ed.)

The Found Object Imagines a Life: New and Selected Poems
Mary Catherine Harper

Naming the Ghost
Emily Hockaday

Mourning
Dokubo Melford Goodhead

Messengers of the Gods: New and Selected Poems
Kathryn Gahl

After the 8-Ball
Colleen Alles

Careful Cartography
Devon Bohm

Broken On the Wheel
Barbara Costas-Biggs

Sparks and Disperses
Cathleen Cohen

Holding My Selves Together: New and Selected Poems
Margaret Rozga

Lost and Found Departments
Heather Dubrow

Marginal Notes
Alfonso Brezmes

The Almost-Children
Cassondra Windwalker

Meditations of a Beast
Kristine Ong Muslim

Praise for

Do Not Feed the Animal

"Alluring like 'a panda with boba,' Hikari Leilani Miya brings forth the razzle dazzle, 'a shining bag of hershey's kisses beneath the chicken breasts,' and punches you in the face. It's beautiful, it's rainbows, it's very big hearts. If you're lucky enough to read it, this book will 'boost your self esteem and all the sea pigs will become turtles.' A ferocious debut ... it has my complete and total endorsement!"

—Michael Chang
author of *Synthetic Jungle*

"Hikari Leilani Miya's *Do Not Feed the Animal* is an incredible debut. She is so good with titles! The titles set the stage for the poems: 'help, i've locked myself inside the moon,' 'vocal ransom note from a witch,' 'i am ready to be your sandwich.' The poems are alive with a beloved albino snake, and San Francisco, and several turtles, and love letters, and the poet's singular voice. Her voice feels immediate, very present, like let's go right now, and we go. I'm neurodivergent and I adore reading neurodivergent poetry like this—associative leaps, incomplete sentences, fragments, lyrics, haiku, ars poetica, self-portraits, list poems, dialectics—and with such a big heart. I wanna be on the sprectrum with the Autistic baddies and Chronic Pain baddies and Anxiety baddies. Have you read our poetry? Buy this book. It's incredible. I feel honored to read about the litany of animals dear to the poet, and all types of nourishment, whether food or fellow beings. Did I mention the poems are funny? Oh, so funny. This collection slays at tricking me into a laugh at a line and then suddenly, a sharp turn into a devastatingly sad line. I've never read a book like this and now I want to read 20 more books just like this. Quite frankly, I love it."

—The Cyborg Jillian Weise
author of *Cyborg Detective*

"Owls try really hard to sound as awesome as Hikari's poems, but they just can't do it. Sorry, owls."

—Kyle Flak
author of *Sweatpants Paradise*

Do Not Feed the Animal

HIKARI
LEILANI
MIYA

POEMS

CORNERSTONE PRESS
UNIVERSITY OF WISCONSIN-STEVENS POINT

Cornerstone Press, Stevens Point, Wisconsin 54481
Copyright © 2024 Hikari Leilani Miya
www.uwsp.edu/cornerstone

Printed in the United States of America by
Point Print and Design Studio, Stevens Point, Wisconsin

Library of Congress Control Number: 2023951975
ISBN: 978-1-960329-35-6

Cover art © Ethan Kocak @blackmudpuppy

Cornerstone Press titles are produced in courses and internships offered by the
Department of English at the University of Wisconsin–Stevens Point.

DIRECTOR & PUBLISHER
Dr. Ross K. Tangedal

EXECUTIVE EDITORS
Jeff Snowbarger, Freesia McKee

EDITORIAL DIRECTOR
Ellie Atkinson

SENIOR EDITORS
Brett Hill, Grace Dahl

PRESS STAFF
Carolyn Czerwinski, Sophie McPherson, Natalie Reiter, Ava Willett

Julia and Richard, for that time we had mochi doughnuts

Linda, for your first time at Waffle Frolic

Tony, for that game hen that was literally on fire

Gentendo_3000 and the66ryder, ramen boys forever even if your topping choices are weird

hoffafsu, do u want spspspspspspghatti for din

DOAhed, do not ever take me through the Bojangles drive thru ever again

& Alfred, for the interesting case involving lemon pepper

Contents

I.

the san francisco fog melting on my tongue.
at home the fog tastes like walnuts

self-portrait as a do not feed the animal sign

the only things preventing me from slapping
a giant red "do not feed the animal" sticker
on my forehead is my pity-me charm and
my insatiable desire for noodles. long noodles, long
life. my life will be more infinite than words lashed to a page.
i slurp them from my spoon. it's a secret not even kept
in my manila file that i can't use chopsticks correctly.

i stare at two lines of poetry until they corrupt my hypothalamus.
telepathically, i order the author to feed me more.
they comply on the next page, white space a horizon,
words like hands outstretched to my tongue and tossed
to the back abyss of my throat.

a tall glass of chocolate pudding is friend-shaped,
not just because pudding is my favorite word. when i nibble
its ear, i roll it around in my mouth, brown body
in an undulating pink bath. by the time i'm nomming
on the tail, my legs have stopped jiggling. eating is
just a transfer of jiggle. i don't bother washing the dishes.
the chocolate carnage grows stale in the sink.

i try to coax marshmallows into my concrete pen.
let's be fluffy together, i say. it's like a saying
i would get in yellow letters on a pink canvas tote bag. the label
says "made in Japan" in japanese. i realize when the marshmallows
have rolled away that i've been talking to the clouds, a hallucination born
out of my starvation and excessive jiggle.

when my professor tries to talk to me on the first day of class,
i point to my graphic tee. it's a picture of a panda with boba and ramen.
i get kicked out of the zoom meeting and surround myself with soft things.
round blobs on blobs. grubhub is blocked. doordash is down. my stomach
growls behind metal bars until a former friend of mine takes pity. he tosses me
a wrinkled gwendolyn brooks. she's never seen again. while the police escort him
away and slap him with a $150 fine, they point to the sign on my locked door:
do not feed the animal

help, i've locked myself inside the moon

i tried to toss the ocean inside of a message bottle,
but the cork popped like new year's, and Moon is whom
i had to answer to. oops. at least her insides are made
of blue cheese. so those who thought you could eat

Moon was right, but you can only eat her insides.
this is the part where you think about what's eating
on your insides, low self-esteem sea pigging about
the low tides of your bloodstream. i'm sorry. just a little.

this isn't an apology because i still believe i did nothing
wrong. i pondered how strange it was that all the oceans
belonged to land, so if there was no ocean for the lands to
claim, then there'd just be more land covered in coral

skeletons and fish bones. do you still want it, i'd ask
as i wave around my ocean-bottle. which lands will get
these salt-dead sands, who decides where borders are drawn
with squid ink and crushed sea shells. tell me, what language

does the dead speak after it has died? if i am going to die here,
alone in this blue cheese moon, will the moon speak for me
or will someone else from somewhere else spoon words
into my funky marbled corpse and pretend there's a heart still

beating? anyways. i'm not saying that you have to, or anyone
has to, but i'd appreciate some help exiting Moon's interior.
maybe if you come, it'd boost your self-esteem and all the sea pigs
will become turtles? i don't have cash, but i can pay in cheese.

being brown in fifteen minutes

i didn't get into harvard but it's not like i was
going to be a doctor anyways. flesh colored band-
ages are just streaks of flour on my bread crust
flesh, nude underwear telling me i'm raw and
unbaked. i didn't know how to use chopsticks
until i was an undergraduate, couldn't speak
beyond *hai* and *tempura udon onegaishimasu* to
fumi-san at her café. i stared down my D+ in
elementary Japanese and it stared back, its gaping
mouth a loud empty watermelon, seedless and sad.

mom still believes that listening to classical music
(the kind i played cymbals and triangle for in orchestra
and pretended i knew on the piano) makes people
smarter. but as much as i listened to the music sharpened
by the spidery fingers of long dead whites while doing
introduction to calculus homework, the highest score i
ever got on those exams was a twenty-eight percent. if
i could take the derivative of für elise and build a fence
around it against the side of a cliff whose side is x, then
maybe i could stop beating my heart with a worn rice scoop.
i've stopped eating white rice. only brown for me.

i can't point out ilocos on a map, can't stomach bloody
pork or lifeless fish eyes. when people ask me if i've been
back, i say *there's no back to return to*. my childhood is
central valley dust and walnut shells, asthma and learning
how to prove my worth in a language that people say should
be my second. say hi in your language, they order. hello,
i say, and they're disappointed that i use white words yet
loathe shakespeare. actually, i don't know who's more
frustrated. where does it hurt, my gym teacher asked me
after a ball hit my chest. she looked me a question when
i said my *suso*. the word vagina startles me, so i still think
pepit. i curl into a ball as i gush thick blood onto a white pad.

eating my gods, all of them

you're a convenience spat from the remnants
of my dreams. between the measures of heat,
salt, fat, and acid that i slice with a dull butcher's
knife, i don't think of the glory graced from
your tongues i shove into mason jars i bought
from walmart. my fascination with your omni-
presence has dissolved in a soup pot boiling
over medium heat for seven minutes. the water
is unsalted, of course. your tears will suffice.
if you bled, it would be a blistered berry cliche.
instead, i'll settle for the ink oozing from pupils,
slurry from your blurred irises. i don't know if
you're enough for an immortal feast. i don't know
if the marrow in your bones will melt in my mouth,
erode my teeth, or allow me to grant my own wishes
without breaking bones with someone i love. this
consumption and preparation is an act of reverence
for you. just don't ask me for the secret ingredient.

22 fillmore bus

music note mask up to my eyes
as kenshi yonezu slithers through

my airpods. fried chicken at o'farrell
fades to green weed by geary street.

warm waffle cones, chocolate-dipped
fingers creep through the bus like sweet

spiders outside the ice cream shop. by loving
cup on union street, sweet becomes

creamy salt waves tinged with cigarette
smoke rolling like tires on the paved streets.

pocket jizo

on working with a teenaged client in ABA therapy

he didn't mean to throw the steak knife past me.
  "when i am frustrated, i can ask for a break."
    he crawls back into his bed and tosses
      the blue comforter over his head.

he shows me the white nanoblocks polar bear i bought at Daiso.
  "can i have something?" he reaches for the bear in my hand.
    on my iPad, i press the IND button for asking
      questions using three words.

he didn't mean to throw the clothes iron at my feet.
  "when I am frustrated, i can ask for a break."
    he sits at his cluttered desk and munches
      on fried chicken until they're bones.

he always plays connect four using the blue pieces.
  "miss kari wins," he says, as the pink and blue clatter
    to the gray plastic tray. on my iPad, i press the ERR button
      for correctly using "you" pronouns.

he didn't mean for his grandfather to fall.
  "grandpa falls because i run very fast."
    he writes the statement down in even letters
      on a blank sheet, using "fell/falls".

i don't show him the round ceramic jizo tucked away
  into my blue cat coin purse. i don't ask "what does miss kari have?"
    he won't say jizo never falls. jizo never fails to smile.
      jizo never speaks or sees.

getting double vaccinated with lawrence ferlinghetti

borrowing lines from Lawrence Ferlinghetti's
Junkman's Obligato *and* Autobiography

i got coney island on my mind,
junkman's obligato flowing
faster through my veins
than flu season antibodies.

are you feeling sick today?
please check boxes one through ten.
enter your date of birth. sign here.

confound the system.
i am going where turtles win

but only after i've eaten
a mochi doughnut from japan-
town. since it's tuesday, there's
no line. something something,

farting trumpets as the third
COVID jab pricks my right
arm. man on the street curses

me out when i refuse to give
him a hug. i take the long way
home, buy a dragon made
of watermelon. i have to pee.

confound the system.
i will miss you, rain over
san francisco. i like it here

and i won't go back
where i came from.

Extinction Burst

noun: in Applied Behavioral Analysis (ABA), an increase
of observed behavior after no reinforcement is given.

I. Extinction burst as an open door

no music, but no silence. machinery snores somewhere unseen.
two isosceles triangles point towards a thick stroke dividing
them; a metallic bar, a starved rectangle guilty and pressured.
press the button. the door doesn't close.
red letters above the door still glow fifteen. the door opens onto
a black and white tiled lobby, polished and shrimp fried rice
scented.
press the button. the door doesn't close.
an electric moment of panic. the door will remain open. is this
better or worse than the door stuck closed between floors, num-
bers flashing nonsensical block lines and floors that don't exist?
press the button. the door doesn't close.
stairs are healthier anyways. but fifteen floors, with how many
little square landings in between angling those dizzying flights
down?
press the button. the door doesn't close.
the button exists as a false sense of accomplishment. when the
door finally closes, a moment of triumph melts into sidewalk
thoughts and petrichor.

II. Extinction burst as seventeen unanswered phone calls

once while you hand your iPad to the mother of her kindergar-
tener dreamily gazing at an abyss-mouthed basking shark in
The Super Shark Encyclopedia. she signs in ASL as you stop
the ringing.
twice while waiting for the 22 bus outside the walking fish poke
bowl restaurant, where the friendly owner always waves hello,
even if he's with a customer.
once as you wash your hands after arriving home. your hands
drip helplessly as the rings and vibrations stretch across the
granite countertops.
after the fifth time, you text your clinical leader again. he's not
stopping, you say.

don't answer, he replies.
the phone rings again. you put your phone on do not disturb.
when you look at your phone again, some hours later, you see
nine missed calls.
once more as you shovel canned ravioli into your mouth before
your 5:30pm session.
again five minutes before session.
at exactly 5:30, you open your zoom meeting. you ask the guilty,
fifteen-year-old face in front of you why he called you seven-
teen times before session, even after the clinical leader answered
once.
he says, hesitantly, that he wanted to tell you something.
what is it, you ask.
after a leaded silence, he replies
i forgot.

III. Extinction burst as disordered eating

at the grocery store, she buys a succulent in a yellow pot instead
of bread or cheese.
when she gets home, she steps on the scale and sees the red line
exactly at 100.
she takes a laxative. then another.
after using the bathroom, she steps on the scale and sees the red
line exactly at 100.
she goes out for a run around the neighborhood. listens to my
chemical romance uphill. green day downhill.
after she showers and dries her hair, she steps on the scale and
sees the red line exactly at 100.
for dinner she has an apple with a tablespoon of peanut butter.
a half hour later, she is bent over the toilet, her hair crumpled
behind her head.
she steps on the scale and sees the red line exactly at 100.
she takes a laxative. then another.
she goes into a restless sleep. in her dreams she is jogging
through a mansion in which all the inhabitants are succulents.
when she wakes up, she steps on the scale and sees the red line
at exactly 100.
not once does she think that the scale is broken.

self-portrait as a grocery store

there are no policemen guarding my sliding glass doors
poster-less because there are no missing children
or lost dogs around

my edges i am green. slim. could you call me
ripe? but in my belly i am carbs.
my heart frozen

pizza and gourmet ice cream. my bladder filled with tea and coffee,
not the kind from starbucks. minute microwave brown rice
is in the same section as asian

and mexican foods. furikake, achuete, fenugreek seeds pepper
the culinary imagination more than what bobby flay can
in a half hour episode of smack talk and flambe.

non-classical piano music drifts through hidden speakers
(not like anyone walks into me with their eyes skyward).
the manager is too embarrassed

to play j-pop or k-pop or even despacito
because anything with a voice is enough
to crack through the breaking of pangea

of frozen peas within the bag. a single mother squints
at the ingredients on macaroni and cheese. she doesn't bother
to read the "cheese" list in parentheses as she tosses three boxes
into her loaded cart. she doesn't see her only boy
quietly bury a shining bag of hershey's kisses
beneath the chicken breasts.

an old man calls me super, like the hero stickers
teachers placed in the corners of A+ exams, while the college student
who just buys a bottle of windex and a box of tissues says i'm

convenient. he passes through the self-checkout and crumples
his receipt into the garbage full of other receipts and water cups.
no one tosses around the word "cheap," because like

"cheese," there are always notes in the parentheses.
free-range. organic. no rBst's, although there's really no difference
between animals with and those without. a yoga teacher laughs

at the words "all natural" on a pack of cookies.
you could package my ass and it'd be all natural, too.
she circles back around to get them before heading to the checkout.

just after closing time, the piano music stops so the janitors
can walk their mops like dogs down the aisles humming songs
they wish their mothers had taught them. maybe

one day, their hearts will be as open as the sliding doors
when someone hungry walks in. some day they will nourish.
some day, they will sing about love. and it will be all natural.

blues in brown

dusty hawk flies south over
muddy mouth of the ditch.
i search for happiness in silent
gossamer horizons of spider
webs stretched across dead
grass. i peek under rocks
to ask the toads but they've all
gone away for winter. tablets for
the dogs' joint pains are dirty moon
wafers, their treats snapped
in half are thick cardboard.
in the silence i ponder generosity.
the sound of a bell like a single
star in a smoggy sky. and i realize
it is one half of an unshelled walnut.
never whole.

roommate in a forty-gallon glass box

the selfishness of glass. made for pairs of eyes
that can see through, into, outside. ignoring
the leaded past. my friend once worked in a lab
where scientists placed glass domes over the brains
of mice, as if seeing their dreams pulse like frantic
demons exposed to dawn could equal some kind
of equation that us humans could magnet on our
refrigerators next to postcards and grocery lists.

what can i say about the roommate? he sleeps, glassy
eyes open, irises gold from the glory of legends
that vibrate along his pale belly. he dreams of those
mice stories where he was feared and revered and left
to ponder whose mercy he would grant today. not like
there is anyone to grant mercy to, not even me, for
his fangs are the tips of needlepoint pens so thin
he's best off using the voice he doesn't possess
to gift me his thoughts: hunger. heat. have a seat.

he doesn't twitch his nose at the barbecued elevator,
numbers red up to eighteen. he's never climbed a tree
yet resides where living pine needles can never touch.
most days he waits for our eyes to meet through glass,
shallow gold moons drinking into the agelessness of
coffee. the encounter happens faster than he can strike
a mouse. it doesn't matter to predators whether or not
prey ever had a chance to open their eyes. maybe that's
why his eyes are always open. so chance is always fair.

i'd like to think that there is mercy between the fork
of his black tongue, a silent fluttering ribbon tasting
the fragility of the american dream: driftwood and pine
scented candle, creased streets littered with crushed cans
and crumpled face masks, three-day old kitty litter and
frozen dinner. mice for him, beef broccoli for me. both
boxed and bagged for our convenience. his eyes are just
sharp enough to make out the rain falling outside. liquid
glass he'll never taste, the freedom to be clear and frigid.
the moon is a tasteless dream. starlight imperceptible to
diurnal pupils that gleam cunningly in my own dreams.

cherries

ripped off the verdant stem
with my teeth   sliver
of peeled skin blushing
faint enamel   tapering
like a hangnail

depths of red gush easily
into my mouth   a wound
a gaping gash sliding to a
satiating ceaseless digestion

tan pit stripped   down
rolled soundly by my tongue,
tapping against my incisors
saying   i too was once
sacred   before emanating
from my lips   an un-
wanted vestigial bone bane
of innocent perfection

i've never had melon bread, but at least i've held a tortoise

while my poet friend contemplates shards of mirror
        and their silvery panes upon pain,
i google melon bread just to see the blockiness of katakana
        on the title of the first recipe
and then i google baby sulcata tortoises because their perfectly crisp
        scores equate to the brown
of a visual crunch. i taste crumbs in my mouth
        through my menstrual dehydration, my body

a desert. i have so much admiration for those animals
        who live in the desert, like camels
that are able to siphon more than fifty gallons of water into their
        hairy hilly bodies within
three minutes. as i sip my water, crunch on the ice, i wonder
        what their atoms remember.
what skies they've rained upon, whose intestines
        they've trickled through. do they remember

being beautiful and teasing the light into rainbows,
        slipping through the flap of minnows' gills,
steaming onto a hotel mirror hours before a bride meets her bride?
        her feet won't sweat in her
heels because she's stumbled blindly through her whole life
        to be able to walk straight down
the aisle to her love without her glasses slipping down
        her beaming face. i've never been to

a wedding but that will change within weeks.
        i'll never have a wedding, but considering its
future absence and the empty space i could fill like a bookshelf
        fills me with victory. instead
i recall my one-time-partner on our one-day-date
        where she came over and we made milk
bread. i called it shokupan, but not in front of her. when she told me
        to knead the dough, i made

quiet whooping noises as i tossed the sticky mass from hand to hand,
        squished it between my
fingers, slammed it onto the floured cutting board. I gently stroked
        the back of it like a baby
tortoise shell—gentle and careful so that jostling wouldn't make it pee.
        she commented on
my technique by not saying anything but *my turn* and deftly shaping
        the dough into a circle.

while it rose in my fridge we rose from my bean bag and stood in line
        at Daiso, where i beeped
and bopped. i wish i could've seen my beaming face beneath my mask
        when she told me i
have great uwu energy. even though we don't talk it's weird to say
        i miss her when we
follow each other on twitter and like tweets
        about eggs with kawaii faces. no one else

has made bread with me. no one else's bread tasted like hers.
        i pass by the japanese bakery
every time i visit japantown. i've never stopped, but sometimes
        i make beeping noises
underneath my mask. when i stand in line at Daiso i think about
        how bread feels while
it's rising, how much space within it isn't bread but we still perceive
        as bread. my bookshelf

is full, but i'm sure i can find space for recipe books i'll never read
        or even cook from. authors
like jet tila and geoffrey zakarian who use ingredients like soy
        and mirin and clarified butter
with their perfect pink chicken breasts. while watching geoffrey
        make risotto on instagram,
i wonder if he's ever made melon bread. if he thinks about tortoises
        while he bakes bread.

love letter to paxton gate

you satisfy my desire for the dryness
of bleached bone, sublimity of serpentine
vertebrae light as breath. to think in each
snake, beneath smooth or keeled scale,
coil simple white wonders bound by muscle
and blood. the grotesque is more in the price
than this gentle remnant of olive life. will you
support my reverence, the confusion of my own
snakes as they slither over a taxonomic relative?

you tickle my whimsy when you pose mice
in hats knocking at a door no one will answer.
chicken in a basket, raccoon head on top another
raccoon head in a forest they'll never see, moss
they've never felt framing their faces with
a pine cone for good asymmetrical measure.

you amaze me with diaphonized wet kitten fetuses,
striking violet and pink streaking through cory
catfish like a permanent sunset bottled in crystal,
a curio for the casually curious. where art and
chemistry bleed into the same vessel, you stain
me with beauty while saluting quiet morbidity.

you provided me with my first zz plant, leaves
so green and glistening my mother thought
they were fake. the scents of burnt bacon,
blistered scallops, and blackened steak
never tainted its sheen as it swooned for years
over my kitchen sink. from your air to mine,

you drain my wallet while filling the american
desire for things, dead things, but i will call them
teaching things for herpetology, zoology, botany.
my atoms may vibrate at a different frequency
than your crystals, but you remind me that
my bones could be bought, my blood can be
bottled, my soul could be sold for $100 plus tax.

jazz

i snip the e off of emotion with a
snap of my fingers—haha, move,
bitch, shake those pear hips to the sound
of rain dancing through cement firmament.
i know i haven't written in a while
but i still slant my *A*'s and *T*'s even when
i'm not paying attention to my *Q*'s because
they just too damn loud. here, i'll send you
a postcard from the fillmore district
of san francisco telling you how much
i miss the swoop of trumpets, the golden
swoon of trombones and the velvet tones
of a bass so deep sharks deep in the bay bob
their blunt blind heads. i click through silence
like a metronome down gum-gray sidewalks
on the way to the post office, raise a glass to toast
those blue-collar workers sending all our
shit saying *wish you were here but not
really!* sforzandos take up so much light
within my head, fireworks poppin' through
late morning mist of petrichor promise—
and man, do i really hate wanting more. but
i'm here to fill this flat world with hills,
no, mountains, the color of my t-shirt dresses
and the flavor of my skin that i ain't letting
no one call burnt. i may be japa-pino, but
there's more beyond my blood that's not
sweet, sass, and sweat. i'll tell you i love you
when i finish my sisney movie marathon
tomorrow night. don't let no one tell you
you can't dance without drums or the moon.

thursday at the office

the day i met the dragon
the sun came up swollen
behind drunk clouds

he sat at his desk
strewn with toys
he wasn't even sure
belonged to him

when he wasn't looking
i popped a candy into my mouth
from the little bag
with a giant yellow caution sign
and japanese i could somewhat read

my eyes full of tears
i inhaled and swallowed
before hurriedly chasing it down
with stale water from my unwashed bottle
and i swear
that was how he breathed
fire

sunset order and raccoon girl

i was sipping a nightmare (0% sweet, extra ice)
when i saw her bushy tail waving out of a putrid green
trash bin. burger king's greasy red sign was buzzing so loud
i couldn't hear the raffle of whopper wrappers or warring pigeons.

warm obsidian eyes. muddy gray shirt. her short fingers grasping
a half-eaten chicken nugget. her ear was torn in one corner—it was
twitching, twitching, always listening. so she heard me say
i'll buy you a sunset. we could even put it in a black garbage bag for you,

to match your eyes. she agreed, so we went into the dingy bar
reeking of tacos and tobacco, adele's voice undulating through patrons
secretly playing pokémon go in corner booths between shots of midnight.
sunset came topped with a smog of cotton candy. she dissolved it immediately,

and for one magnificent moment, a dying swirl of sugar
was more beautiful than the cosmos. raccoon girl dipped her fingers in
and licked them sloppily before downing the sugared sun in a single swig.
tell me, she said, what is the most difficult thing in the world?
her torn ear twitched and twitched. putting on a bra, i told her,
now on my eleventh nightmare (15% sweet, extra boba)
so that's why i only wear sports bras. raccoon girl shrugged and told me
she didn't even know how many nipples she had, though once
her tail got caught on the clasp of some homeless lady's exposed bra.
i don't miss the hair, she said.

outside the sky was redder than the burger king sign.
i waved her goodbye as she caught the 38 bus to target. she didn't pay
her bus fare. i had another nightmare (25% sweet, extra chocolate pudding)
and pondered the great unknown: nipples, bras, burger king.
when i woke up the next morning, a target bag sat on my bed.

ABC's of the american west

apple computers designed in style; west coast
best coast, we've got a lot to boast about. fast
cars driving through another chinatown, american girl
dolls lining window shops saying black lives matter, always and for-
ever. somewhere in the desert we can hear whispers of
flower songs sung by native americans, ancestors
gone but here in spirit, voice, and architecture.
here we sought refuge but were refused, met by
icy stares of those with paler skin and hands like spiders
jailing us in webs of hate. are we free yet? just ask our
kids. generational trauma passes down
like sourdough bread recipes, pinch of starter in the
mead jars of our DNA. so what's
next? farmland stretching for miles, meeting the pacific
ocean in a salt-breeze embrace. on every corner,
pizza kitchens, taquerias, cafes run by sassy black women shouting yaaaas
queen! they crawl up steep hills so that from the top down, we can
run run run in the sun sun sun. come to think of it, the
sunrises are sweeter, the sunsets deeper,
tasting like the hearts of walnuts atop black forest cake.
utopia? upon reflection, manifest destiny was the
vehicle that turned the bold to bitter in our bellies,
wet mouths hungry for more while the homeless sign cardboards in pen:
x o, x o, god bless. anything helps. have any spare change?
yes! change is what the west sees in its reflection, a future that is the
zenith of america's melting-pot society.

too much for sleep

my supernumerary throbs
because my dentist says i
clench my teeth because
i'm stressed because
i'm working eighteen hours a week plus
school and it isn't enough but
it's enough to keep me from
biting my knuckles and
hungering
for *hahaha* affection and anime
movies with gore breaks—

i wish there was no room
for the pain in my half-tooth
or i could suggest it to my
half-dead heart i can call
a joke don't you see i have
more than half a heart stupid—

i'm tired of boys and girls
walking with holes to drink
frappuccinos and holes just
have slush poor out of them
and holes that drain to sludgey
oceans and i'm tired i'm tired—

II.

my skin is very squishy, thank you.
it always has been.

i am once again writing about my skin

because i don't want to tell strangers who ask me where i learned
to speak english and what country i grew up in. i live in the country,
in this country, the one where they ask me why my feet aren't bound
and which ancestor of mine was a geisha. when they ask about
my ancestors, they fail to see how i am connected to a stained
and wrinkled past by more than just sinew and cells. the water
that nourished them, that fell from the sky to moisten
their parched mouths and gave them fluidity to speak,
erodes mountains. is it remarkable or disturbing that we can dig up
a weed from any other country, put it in a white ceramic pot
shaped like a hedgehog, then sell it for $15? i see myself
in a boutique window planted in soil that's supposed to be mine,
and i'm supposed to thrive, sunless, without knowing
where i'm supposed to belong.

i dreamt again of the thin-lipped white woman who told me
the reason why i don't appreciate jane austen is because my skin
is like spiced tea instead of cold milk. pride and prejudice slips
off my shoulders like a shawl in the wind because, dear, their love
is just different, and maybe one day you'll see the value in romance.
what do i say when people ask me what i am? i want to say,
i'm just like you, only shorter in stature, bigger in spirit.
i want to say i escaped the torments of the past, and that makes me
more resilient than even i understand.

i want to say i am loved. instead, i tell them why my skin is the color
of barely-there forest paths known only by deer and kitsune.
with every truth i write, the tikbalang and baku dancing delicately
beneath my skin emerge and weave themselves amongst my lines.
can you see them? they may elude you today, but one day, dear,
you may come to understand their love and what it means
to be invisible in your own home.

i am ready to be your sandwich

my middle name rhymes with salami,
and i'm just as salty. please don't
toast me. no roast beef here, but
there are thin slices of swiss cheese
i wrote on like parchment with whole
grain mustard. now let's talk about greens:
curly crunch of kale. sharp snap of iceberg
lettuce almost crisp enough to cut your
tongue. don't worry, i won't do that. i hope
this is enough for you. i've been marinating
for so long, it's like being forgotten
at the crusts of a dream torn by your fingers.

aren't your feet cold?

for my great-aunt sumi (sue) mitsuyoshi

thanks for asking, auntie sue. but it's 75 degrees in here
        and our omniscient carpet has never

held a fiber of frigid. can i have another kool-aid burst,
        the red one? mom never lets us drink

those things. i forgot whether the kool-aid man says *oh yeah!*
        or *ka-pow!* as he bursts through

a brick wall, but even though you don't know his penciled grin,
        he appreciates your money and i

appreciate your thin frame dainty on our sofa as you watch
        my cherry-stained fingers place

littlest pet shop bobbleheads into their little nooks and crannies.
        when i am old enough to

babysit ally (do you remember how much you adored her wispy hair,
        the pudge of her cheeks?)

i will tell her about you. she doesn't remember.
        i will put socks on her feet though she's not cold.

self-portrait as an *Andrias japonicus*, ideally with a hat

when i think about all the things people want me to be, like
sitting straight with my legs crossed, dutiful daughter folding
clothes with deft fingers, i turn scarlet and slimy. i think instead
about what it means to be female guarding a den instead of going

out to look for one that suits me. there will be plenty of space
for plants, shiny rocks, moss balls. some squishy things here
and there. i have lots of male friends that drift in and out
to bring me arare and yu-gi-oh cards. and when they leave, i'm free

to follow. i want to be one of those creatures whose hat
is permanently attached to her head, so when a man shakes me
upside down or any which way i still have protection from the sun
and his stupidity. if i had ear holes, my hat would cover them

so that i wouldn't have to hear anyone asking me to repeat myself,
especially my mom when i tell her it's okay to work out in shorts
and a sports bra. how it's okay to lift the katana above my head
because my torn chest muscles have healed. and really, who wouldn't

want a permanent hat? maybe the katana could be optional. the weight
and flow of the river makes me consider form and shape without
being ashamed of my size or my fat or my flesh. i peacefully meander
around for weeks before eating a snail. there are no clothes to fold.

the haunting of fish eyes

at first i wrote because my dreams penned beauty:
kaleidoscope of
  pink tumbles softly to grass
    each petal: brushstroke.

and then, to answer a question stemming from nightmare:
  when does a rapist
    stop being a rapist—when does he
      become an ex-rapist, if ever?

what i wanted to say didn't fit on a postcard.
  when is it too late to write
    to the dead? i wish, on one thousand
      paper stars, you, and you, and you were here.

everything i said on a postcard haunted me.
  i'm at Pine Flat with dad and great-uncle ray.
    the houseboat works today. but we're not
      doing catch-and release. there's a blue icebox.

later, because i abandoned my appetite:
  yellow moon-eyes lifeless on ice.
    white bony flesh steam on my china plate.
      i was too cowardly to save any of them.

i didn't close my mouth around their bodies, so i ate my words:
  does sunlight still dance
    on the scales of slaughtered ghosts,
      can their eyes behold their gods?

and when i swallowed:
  to whom do i owe an apology—
    to the ones who will never understand,
      or the one who feasts upon forgiveness?

i wrote because i couldn't sing my farewell to innocence.
  white kitsune plushie tumbles off my bed,
    lands on tangled wires that connect my tired eyes
      to a history of haunting, to hunger, to every bleeding fish heart.

RE: childhood

in this one the cockatiels don't die.
rather, i don't see the death as an end
but as gray wings feathered against white.
crackers would have learned to ride on my shoulder
and pinch sunflower seeds from my lips. he'd even tweet his name.

instead of watching, i swallow humility, a pill without water,
tie a stripeless white belt around a uniform
my hair in a bun i've done myself,
learn to punch my fist to my steel in the mirror.
when the instructor asks me if i've found god,
i'll tell him that i have. he was hiding underneath the couch.

when i give great uncle kay's funeral,
i pause when people laugh instead of barreling through panic,
wondering why people laugh at a memory when the body forgets it.
i lose myself in the echoes of buddhist chants instead of loose threads
of black against my jostling thighs.

i know so many languages, like how the boy in my fifth grade class
knew so many types of cheese. my name is the same in all of them.
i ask for a hair tie from my mom in illcano. i know exactly how many boxes
of advil were found with auntie rose's body.
i can order churros and carnitas tacos at the monday sale in spanish.
r's roll off my tongue and gather as sugar scree at the base of a mountain
made of pan dulce. i can write to my aunt in japanese: hiragana, katakana,
and even kanji, all with the correct stroke order. her tongue doesn't isolate her.

i see a therapist. i learn how to swallow antidepressants like
how i would swallow my desire for an end. i cry every time i see her
until all that comes out is salt. i use it to season my filet mignon,
cooked in a buttered iron skillet to a medium.

in this one i say i want to be a veterinarian instead of a forensic scientist
and i'd actually ask for help when the equations and formulas
became confusing. in this one i find out my iq score and beat it
with my drumsticks. i win a trophy. i stop reading and pretend
to empathize with poets. this poem is never written.

elegy for a future nutritionist

how does a teenaged dream die?

with my lips against the glossy sheen
of a honeycrisp apple. perfect painted fire
smooth against my tongue. my definition
of perfection as a bodily balance:
the stomach and heart in a loving ouroboros.

with a bite i didn't take out of a white apple.
the slim macbook pro everyone in class had
covered with millennial pink cases. i scribbled
in my notebook as the professor flashed through
slides. did i learn that? am i supposed to know that?

with ninety-five calories, some 2.5 from fat,
each counted like pennies or seconds measured
by each academic semester and thin hand. of course
i see the irony. i say, eat this. i deprive myself of that.
i moved the apple from my desk to my mini fridge.

with the acknowledgment it wasn't ripe, i wasn't
ripe, i wasn't right for this kind of growth, the twists
of my serpentine mind recoiled in nonplussed misery.
did all 800 students really understand stoichiometry
on day two? how general is this chemistry?

with every passing season, a dependence on words—
my own voice in sync with the drubbed seed in my core
beating red, orange, yellow, instead of glass beakers, burners,
burn from failure. were i to write my memoir at that point,
consuming sonnets and odes, i could almost call it perfection.

with the struggle of transformation, a withered skin
sheds like tears. tears: there were so many, salt withered
my cheeks. this is my ecdysis. i keep my paper skin coiled
in a bamboo box to remind me: count lines, not grams.
i ate the entire apple for breakfast. it was harshly delicious.

omamori (御守)

i am love radiating within silken silence,
luck tucked gently into the flat dark,
safety swinging to *american pie*

on your rearview mirror. the gods
blessed a piece of themselves after
being blessed with mochi and oranges.

don't open me if you love me. keep
my mouth closed until i am ready
to burn and become spark, smoke, ash.

in which the potato writes the future

show me the unloved and i'll show you
a poem. it lacks petals even though it is
not yet winter. i separate the duck bills
from yellow paper folding fans, china
town from porcelain blue bowls. there
is the scent of blue smoke, serpentine
in a gray sky. i won't tell you what
the poem is about or even if i love you.
why is it important for you to know, and
where would you keep those words?

the poem can stand yet chooses to sit
on a bench against the wall next to the
mochi doughnut shop, not in line because
scent satiates. it has a clear plastic flask
from the dollar store that holds water. it
deflects stares. absorbs night and time.
holds the annoyance of an early sunset
in its hands like a raccoon with fresh
garbage, only it stays undipped in water.

its third head has its eyes permanently
closed. all its ears are pierced with hoops
and sparkle. potato, it thinks. potato. potato.
potato. fat. famine. french fries. eyes bored
out of their minds, stomachs round but
empty. there is no story, the compass
needle spins and spins in the dance of
all directions. though it asks how and why
it is not beyond what. so it sits and sips
and thinks i would like. i would like
you better, maybe, if you just shut up.

agnostic cockroaches

> *"to be clean is to be good, in America"*
> *–Natalie Diaz*, that which cannot be stilled

we say nana like tanned surfer slang: *nah brah*.
in her poor oahu home, slick porphyry tiles cut
into perfect squares support the broken dusty piano,
the plastic covered furniture that marks with a sweaty
film when brown bare legs spread across the seat. atop

cabinets *periplaneta americana* antennae prick paper
plates with leftover lumpia. no one knows why nana feeds
them when she has seven children, dozens of grand-
children who visit daily. when did i last visit? when
tata was still alive, when i was still scared to let

my foot touch the rag rope bath mat because
when i was four i saw ants traversing the soft rainbow
braids and my flesh only knew white walls and white carpet.
the geckos hide and i seek them as they scamper across screen
doors. i hide and the cockroaches seek my mochi crunch crumbs

beneath the thick dining room table that could belong in a museum.
across the fence i seek tata ventura's spirit in the chameleons
camouflaging in the orchids above the outdoor stainless steel sink.
i can only sense the reptilian green amongst floral brightness. please,
i think to them, eat the cockroaches. take their lives, but leave nana's.

i'll be blunt. the faded jesus altar at the end of the short hall
freaks me out. his pale hands spread to the plates of untouched
pancit below. some hours later cockroaches appear. they are gods
who worship no god, eating beneath a god. come out, geckos.
come visit, chameleons. that's tata ventura's food. i don't hear light

vibrations of their singing wings as they crawl back into dark
crevices to sleep and breed in the brown foundations of faith.

double sonata for the post-apocalypse

movement I
i can't feel gravity but i can feel her pulling
blood down my inner thigh, pooling beneath
my white-socked heel. no pads. no pressure.
no plants thirsting for water when their roots
draw out the last of red life from black soil.

movement II
a black bear pushes her claws through
a sealed box of apples. the scent of ferment
taints the air with the state of survival:
yellow and brown, sealed away, but not
impenetrable. enter: the sound of teeth
sinking through softened sunset peel.

movement III
i walk through the woods looking down
for the heads of mushrooms defying and thriving
on decay. i once had a profile picture of a frog
squatting on top of a red-capped mushroom.
his eyes bulged out from either side of his head,
but no one will ever meet that gaze again or care.

movement IV
music dictates that scars must be sung. knifemarks
that scored bark seal. roads become dust, the shadows
on dirt mark the time. pale wounds crisscrossing
shoulder blades remind me to look up and find the moon
because that's what i'm supposed to do when it's night
or dark or hopeless. i am no longer drawn to light.

movement V
the irony of spiders' webs representing human vanity
is not lost on the spider. up high in the pine tree that
no one will ever strike again for sap or gold, she spins

a new tale for her hundreds of unhatched babies:
in this new era, vanity is a painted wooden noun
of the past. so many eyes glisten in the dark.

movement VI
if i were currently beginning the song about end times,
there would be fire, and somewhere in the middle there
would be floods and grinding of glaciers. because i am
in the end and not sure where or how end it is, i will end
by crushing a blue sheet of paper in my hand. when i uncurl
my fingers, the sharp breath of rot succumbs to gravity.

loving Morris from *Shang-Chi and the Legend of the Ten Rings*

love poems scare me because i am scared to be loved, to feel
a blue or gold glow in my chest when i behold a body i perceive
as beautiful. but when i saw you, i was smitten by your chaotic goodne

just because you have no face doesn't mean that you can't be cute
or loved. no one knows how you know that the forest eats trespassers
when no one has seen you eat a mango or dumpling or egg. do you even eat

maybe your pavonine wings don't work, maybe some people are disturbed
by your extra set of stout legs that remind them of biting creepy crawlies.
but how can one not love your bumbling, fried chicken wing body

as you scamper across the Ta Lo grass and play dead like a dog? your antics
are ageless. your blobbiness beholds innocence greater than a child told
to go inside by his mother. thank you for letting me love
all of your furry mysteries.

brown girl nadir

maybe the poem begins when i am birthed from dirt
that sprouts walnut trees. every nut a nickel. each
of my neophyte fingers a song stuffed into thick gloves
stained black. i press a cloth to my mouth as dust swirls.

maybe the poem begins when there was a rock scraped
against my twelve-year-old wrist. white ash down a branch.
when the rock became scissors, no one noticed. when ash
became viscous ruby, no one cried. there were knives. then none.

maybe the poem begins when i run the slowest leg of the girl's relay.
my stride nearly half of the slender deer legs flying past. when coach
told me after another asthma attack that maybe i should find a different
sport. or stick to marching band. baton transmogrifies to vibraphone keys.

maybe the poem begins when my mom asks if i need to see a therapist
because i wasn't raised to love other women, not that way, *not in
this house where ain't nobody crazy* and maybe eventually i'll stop drinking
in the scent of girls' hair when i drink down pills i apparently don't need.

maybe the poem begins when i am raped. again.
maybe the poem begins when he's found not responsible.
maybe the poem begins when i stand at the cusp of a yawning gorge.
maybe the poem begins when i fly home with red swollen eyelids.

maybe the poem will never begin, words muffled inside the dark shells
of walnuts, drowned in the verdant icy waters of a gorge, pounded
out on marimba keys and timpani drum heads like some kind of heart-
beat. i sign my quiet noise with a $5.95 black pen i sold for my soul.

what are you reading

& what is it saying   about me

about my sloppy   handwriting

does it say if ink   breathes

easier than water or   honey

& what about your   ink

does it sleep like   night

on your skin   paler

than sun ripened   bones

& does it give the   recipe

for fried chicken or   chicken skin

or how to make puppy   stickers

and are those words   unimportant

III.
光

(aka i hope you have time for this poem)—

it's been a while since you've written a poem
  or arranged the sonnet, with arranging cut up lines
  on your living room floor.
it's been a while since you've wandered through 日本町
  in your flip flops you've worn
  since high school graduation. tell dad it was worth the $18.
it's been a while since you've worn a novel halloween costume
  even though you bought three pokémon onesies last year
  and decided they were too hot.
it's been a while since you read tarot cards, letting the king
  of swords slip out while sloppily shuffling. (remember when
  you'd leave out a silver mug for the goddess artemis because
  you always wanted to be a virgin with a big big bow and you
  are only half of that)
it's been a while since you texted your brother
  (because instagram likes don't count):
  here's my podcast. pls share with your friends. pls share my pictures
  like how mom used to make us share those jarred belgian chocolate
  truffles from costco.
it's been a while since you've bought new underwear,
  or worn a headband, or used a full-size sanitary pad,
  or touched something violently pink and fluffy. but–
tonight you read a poem to your partner. this morning
  you introduced a multi-genre project to 38 undergraduates
  with no questions asked. and–
last night you popped pills past your lips instead of putting
  a blade to your wrist,
  and slept like you weren't afraid of dreams.

bedtime story for the me who saw [█████████]

feat. shirley the suspended cymbal for every [█████████]

i'm reciting this from under your thin pillow
that smells like l'oreal tear-free shampoo,
remnants from your tangled garden
of wakame hair that made you cringe
when it hit your back out of the bath.

your hair is straight kelp now. full of tears. if
it makes you feel better, the tears are from
the eye(s) of [█████████]. when you say
"i love you," twenty years from now,
you'll mean it like how you love marie
callender's chicken pot pie. he won't.

it's good you hate the number nine now
because when title ix tells you he gets
his degree and you don't even get your
dignity, you're going to stand on the pier
and think about much you can be
for a sea lion, for how long, how cold

the sea is that you welcome into your lungs.
more than you ever were for him. consider
the word *used*. [█████████] can't use you
like how use of that fat yellow ticonderoga
left a permanent fleshy blister on your
rosy right middle finger. you'll also use that.
he can't use you anymore. you're not used.

it's not october yet, so i won't horrify
you too much. you switch to biolage
shampoo. you still use white bars of
dove soap. [█████████] is contained
by a small white pill whose name
you adore. you stop adoring your
name, for good. you are no longer
living in your own [█████████] nightmare.

ROY G BIV as do not pass go, do not collect $200

prologue

white door closes when i'm yanked wailing from the womb.
white towels don't wipe the brown from my skin.
white walls swaddle me in an innocence that evaporates when i see the sun.
white pain floods behind my eyelids as i tell my mother i'm not hungry.
my stomach eats itself into white.

I

red door closes because i'm too slow at picking my own token. i wanted
the dog, but it's taken and i wouldn't be able to put it down anyways.
my brother is always the car. pot of gold went mysteriously missing. i
balance the hat on my pinky, run over my bare toes with a wheelbarrow.
my blood. soiled.

II

orange door closes because princeton university said i didn't belong
in new jersey. i still made friends there anyways, tuned and beat a bass
drum with the orange/black plaid, straw boat hatted people who told
me i could sit with them even though i was red. i can't buy this space,
only polaroid the memory. is this the $200 i was looking for?

III

yellow door closes because i'm the wrong kind of asian, my ume knees
dried and salted, mochi cheeks toasted and warmed even in the center
of new york blizzards. what does it mean when i can't use my tongue
the way i'm supposed to, when i don't even know the brushstrokes for
love, happiness, or snakes?

IV

green door is locked with my key. i peer through the peephole and
see walnut orchards, summer corn waving goodbye because i know
if i open the door the trees transmogrify to rustic wall decorations at
italian restaurants and pier one imports. green properties were always
so nice, but never truly mine.

V

blue door locks because i can't sing *let it go* with the little girl who has black bangs like mine. i see her underwear lines through her pink tights and i wonder who will forgive me for looking. the orange card says to pay a fine instead of going to jail, but i pay in books and polished stones.

VI

indigo door locks because even though it's my favorite color, i can't swallow it due to salinity and sorrow, alcohol and aversion to light. every pill i take is supposed to be a light in my belly, but lurks like a mountain on a dark horizon.

VII

violet door closes because i haven't dated enough girls. girls to me are ghosts: easy to see, difficult to understand. none of them want to haunt me, even though my house has enough cobwebs and snakeskins and little dead things sitting on my dusty shelves. i kept $200 in a box disguised as a book, but the last time i checked, only my passport is there. i roll the dice and move six spaces. on the way, i say "i wish i could stop here" until i remember i'm broke and so far away from Go.

epilogue

black door opens for everyone except the blackbirds, because they're not corvids. i ask them, how does that make you feel? but they continue pecking at things i can't see at the gnarled trunks of london plane trees. i put on my hat and leave the square.

why yes, thank you for noticing

my name, sharp light
on your soft tongue
peppered with all
the jeweled ikura
brine-pickled embers
just waiting to pop.

you roll my name
in a bamboo makisu,
squeeze the excess
into your egg for that
umami japanese flair.

how pretty, how unique, how
cool as a kokeshi expression
inked on moth winged wood,
kimonos stamped with sakuras
blushing brighter than kamaboko.

you don't see the brown in me,
the lumpia-crunching, i-don't-eat-out-
of-pots-so-i-don't-get-pregnant-me.
so you don't ask anak, how are your aunties
in ilocos? you don't know about the math facts

homework crumpled beneath my pillow
the night before my first grade math
test. you don't know why we don't
put our purses on our ground, you
don't understand the hawaiian salt
and garlic hidden beneath my bed.

you don't know why you don't know
my name. my skin. the depth of brown
in my eyes, my blood some ungodly
percentage of shoyu.

beyond the dusting of mochiko flour,
the sweet earth of an beans, crackling
that could be my nori or my hair, i am
especially that sprinkle of diversity on your pie
chart, that bamboo mat and ceiling,
waterproof, sleek, green, and unbearably
light.

unsent letter to my samurai ancestor

September 24, 2020

i don't know your name, but
your warrior blood flows through my veins
but chilled and hollow like 木枯らし[1]—
though we have air conditioners
to keep us shivering
i shudder at the thought
of your blade at someone's
neck, the pinpoint of an arrow
in someone's eye like our family
crest: 見矢[2] and something
about three circling arrows that 婆ちゃん[3]
buried or burned because this nation
declared us traitors—

i've probably failed
your legacy because my words
are 何でもない[4] and unpublished—
unpolished like my short year in kendo
your language partly lost on my tongue
because i skipped too many university classes
to sleep and dream about the 勇婦[5]
i could be elsewhere—

i'd say ごめんなさい[6]
but i don't expect you to forgive

_____

[1] *kogarashi*, the cold wind that blows at the end of autumn
[2] *Miya*, the atypical kanji spelling of my last name whose symbols
represent an eye and arrow
[3] *baachan*, translates to "grandmother" but in this case refers to my
great-grandmother
[4] *nandemonai*, or nothing special
[5] *isamu fu*, heroine
[6] *gomennasai*, an informal way of saying "sorry" with the expectation
of forgiveness

my laziness and my weak lungs—
how i wish there would be some
魔法 糸 [7] to connect us
even if you didn't believe in magic
or envision microwave tamales
i bear your name—
光 見矢 [8]

---

[7] *mahou ito*, magic thread
[8] *Hikari Miya*, the characters of my name; not reversed because I am
Japanese/Filipino American

hello legacy

i run my fingers down the supple spines of your back—
solemn stalagmites rising and falling with your dark breath.

keep guarding your piles of clouds that will never fall
as rain. i like you better amongst all the damp gray,

although i wish you would open your eyes at some point.
i'd love to witness their wonder, cry memories with you

that echo through the damp i've forgotten is dreadful.
i wish i could look into your face, fearless and full

of promise. hello legacy, i'd say. i'm here to claim you
but not slay you, parade you like pink promises kept

past sunset, balance your name on the tip of my tongue
like a knife. but now that i am here with you, i know

that the best cure for disappointment is a teaspoon of
acacia honey and eternal rest. i inhale the miasma

of our tomorrow before my hand slips off the place
where your tail should have been. i fill the wound

with dragon scales still dreaming of their splendor.
hello legacy. sleep well and remember the taste of honey.

self-portrait as a frozen banana

you real banana, yeah?
i can see it in peoples' gazes
on the islands when they talk
to me. even though i can pronounce
kama'āina correctly, i'm shamefully
caught when i call *shave ice*
a *snow cone.* even though i order
the lychee flavor, not tiger's blood
like normal on the mainland.

i'm below zero and maybe too ripe,
past the spotting stage and just brown
and beyond frigid. maybe i'd be good in moist
banana bread, the one my mom always
made with walnuts from our farm.

on the inside im not even yellow asian,
just white, because i write books and poems,
i use words like *posit* and *clandestine* and
rhinella marina when i see the invasive cane
toads flattening themselves like deflated sugar-
less malasadas at my sister's townhouse complex.

when i return to the mainland (but why is it
the mainland?) no one cares about being
banal, but they're fascinated by by my accounts
of saimin that i leave the kamaboko off of.

everywhere i go it seems no matter what
my temperature, no matter how numb i can make
someone's fingers when they touch me, there's
always someone out there ready to eat me
dead, alive, frozen, thawed, unpeeled.

i set out to write greatness, or something like that

in 2017 when i had overdosed on ativan, i dreamt,
or actually i wrote, the best poem the world had
ever seen. *this will win me millions, all the awards,*
i thought in my dark, dizzy stupor. whether it was
3 a.m. or 3 p.m. didn't matter, time wouldn't matter
when people read this amazing poem of mine.

when the overdose was over, i checked the notes
on my phone. the world's best poem! it had to be
there! and there it was, words splattered across
the dark of the screen... and so that was it, the start
of my foolishness.

so it was there i ended. i woke up, really woke up, and just
cried into my navy pillow until the wet spots were black
as the past shadowy days, maybe years. years later,
when i was watching snow glitter on the slopes as puffy
neon jackets snowboarded and skied over and out of sight,
a girl with hair reminiscent of a dying flame, who told me
she had just taken a lot of mushrooms, slid me a card. no,

it wasn't her business card. The Tower, it read. URIEL.
The Fire of God. Transformation. *sorry, i thought you would
like this, it reminded me of you,* she said, before hurrying
off to shed her two pairs of jeans, because she was going to
ski for the first time. i flipped the card over and over, as if
a poem would just appear before me, as if Uriel, his hands
full with weapons, would hand me a bunch of words and say
*hey girl! i know you've had rough life, so here's the meaning
of poetry, here's who you are and what you were meant to do,
here is all your potential greatness all clearly stated in this song
i stole from God himself, even though i know you don't believe
in him, he wrote one just for you, wouldn't you like to know
how special you are? how much everyone will soon adore you?*

i'd like to say i've grown from trying to die quietly in navy
bedsheets, and from attracting all sorts of wonderful weirdness
on the side of a mountain, but even if i haven't achieved much
in that span of time, at least i know i can go out to the lake and sit
on a swinging park bench and listen to the sound of duck feet on gravel.

origins

my name crawled out
from beneath a kotatsu

before i even knew
what a kotatsu was.

outside was filthy white
but i didn't feel any chill.

i wasn't exactly nameless.
i was shadow shapeless.

it found me sitting
by the open classroom

door. i was eating
cheerios out of a ziploc

as it hopped into
my cardigan pocket.

at night i soaked it
in a deep hot bath

its pores leaking light
warmer than honey.

ars poetica as not reading poetry

i'll do it tomorrow. i'll just stack
these books nicely in a line
on my living room coffee table
so that visitors think i'm cultured.

i'm too busy. i talk a lot for someone
who doesn't think in complete sentences.
it's too hard to write in complete sentences.
i think in lines, blocks, shapes, colors, song.

i need to do chores. i'm not sure when
the dryer decides that my clothes are dry
enough but it's never enough. i should just
get a clothes line to stretch across my life.

i need to feed my animals. never mind
that my kitty can't see in a straight line
and the others can't slither into an
ouroboros. every body needs sustenance.

i need to eat and words won't fill me up
the way my homemade beef pho will.
i love when the straight pale noodle lines
fold into squiggles, and fold into my stomach.

IV.

florida man is never an asian girl
but yet the alligators persist

一寸先は闇（いっすん さき は やみ）

proverb translation: darkness lies one inch ahead

for every dollar i spend on plastic
frogs and thin squares of washi paper
i can feel my mother breathing down
my neck hairs how i'm going to die
a poor poet in a cardboard box.
at least i will have a box, i think
as i buy another box of yu-gi-oh cards.

i definitely don't have a problem,
i think as i put green bath toy turtles
into my fat cat bookstore tote. i need
to keep up my appearance, i need
three of the same hat but all different
colors, and three large buttons to pin
onto the side so no one steals them,

so i do this to confuse thieves—they see
so many colors, they just gape, give up
hope, and choose to not smash the car
window because rainbows are not
valuable. if someone touches my
backpack i hear an infinite jingle
of my hatted blue whale shark—*hey!*
i am being stolen, like, right now!

there's no way i cannot be successful,
because i have a costco membership, and
dad has a costco membership, so
how can he expect mediocrity when
i need blueberry muffins the size of my head?
even if i live in a costco box, it's the best
damn box in town that still smells
of unripe bananas or fluffy hot dog buns.

and what of the books! mom, ALL
of them are for my thesis. my thesis
is very big. i need these books because
at any given time i am reading, especially
when i walk down south monroe street
right in front of the capitol building, so
when all those old white men who want
nonwhite studies to not be things look
out their stupid victorian windows lined
with velvet cream curtains and see me,
a brown girl reading brown girl things,
they wonder if they should further rob me
as i walk directly into a signpost
celebrating florida's diverse history,

because sometimes after i feed my kitty at 3:27 a.m
i like to sit on the cold floor of my bathroom.
i cannot tell it is white in the dark. i
like it in there because there are no things
i can see, no rainbows or plastic turtles. no
words to read or pages to turn one way or
another. if i got in the tub marked with
a footprint i can't scrub away, i could cry
and imagine what's filling the dark from
my eyes is all the money i spent that day.
mom, look! it all paid off! i'm very happy now.

on sundays i tell my opponent we are
using my custom d20s that were $45
each. of course, i have the shiniest, newest
card sleeves, my thick rubber mat unfrayed.
i confidently call the low roll, and as i match
their "i'm going to win" gaze, i say—throw them high.

RE: teens

thank you for shopping at teenage years. please come again!

those weird black and electric blue lima bean shaped vinyl track shoes
that start overheating in 80-degree weather.... $45
        dad said that looked like a good deal, should last me all four
years of high school varsity track and field.... approximately $12/year

being hungry.... free but feels like it costs $17.99
        mom says we have food at home (it expired last year).... free
        thanking my undiagnosed eating disorder.... $1 thank you car
        from the dollar tree
  brother taking my lunch mom packed as i ran math club.... $7-$12
depending on what was left over from dinner

not having social media.... free but costs friends
        asking my friends if something was a meme.... a lot of free
        awkward laughter

not being able to drive anywhere
average price of gas per gallon.... $3.36
average movie ticket price..... $8.13 + XL popcorn
crying about not seeing the lorax with my friends.... free emotional damage
asking who john wick was.... free looks of pity
a large taro boba at the fresno mall
  when we went once or twice a year.... $5 + tax
the asian lady looking me up and down and trying to sell me a small
  because i'm small.... $4.25 + tax

seventeen college applications..... [REDACTED]
cornell university acceptance....
several thousand dollars a semester for four years
plus medical treatment for the involuntary leave of absence....
  [REDACTED]

writing poetry when i was supposed to be doing
  calculus homework…. $0.10/page
my high school english teacher when i gave him everything i wrote
  after graduation….priceless

stress of living in florida…. maybe i'll just settle
  for a pack of cigarettes, if i knew which end to light

city of lost keychains

i wish the concept of losing anything wasn't so ancient or infinite
so that every time a mushroom in a graveyard is lost to the weight
of a horribly gray storm everyone falls to their knees and mourns
mycorrhizae. or like when tallahassee starts tasting like ginger
ale that has lost its fizz everyone books flights to san francisco
and inhales salt and sweet right outside the whirl of baggage claim

but here i am with yet another bag (blue with white and black and red
maneki neko) from which dangles a stainless steel ring and chain
with the last link parted like lips about to take their first sip of hot
(not scalding) cocoa. i take it off and replace stainless steel with
more stainless steel, but this one has a soft witch doctor and maybe
if it falls off i can hear the gentle push of plush as it tumbles against
dry grass or bounces off a dangerously jagged curb. and then there are

broken chains pushed awkwardly beneath my mount of blank postcards
(i swear i'll send one day because the united states postal service works
marvels at delivering my friends sparkly pictures of flowers). i can make
a little abstract pond for my frog figurine with broken chains as steely ripple
in the shape of a lily pad or parts of a curving spine. there's the planchette
dark and scratched and waiting for new jump rings to connect it to
a chain i can salvage from the happy pink cheeked rice cooker or from
that heavy oh so heavy cornell medallion that put years of iron weight
on my keys and my conscious and my academic transcripts saying i suck.

i'm imagining my pink cowboy hat kirby somewhere in the underworld
where persephone dangles him from a long finger and asks darling what
took you so long to get here? everything circular that wears hats always
finds its way directly beneath tallahassee, where the underworld bustles
with government officials who make bad choices about education and
babies. one day i'll make my way down there and find my plastic mint
seal keychain beneath the heel of charon and my pokémon slobbered on
by cerberus. i'll hold up my frog keychain that is growing ever so shorter
but i'll never give up on. i press the button and the lurid light from its
mouth produces a blink everyone marvels at. mechanical ribbits echo. and
echo.

ars poetica as my desk in dodd hall basement

this desk is ageless. years after dusted
years lurking in drawers and stamped
as watermarks on the sliding side table.
someone painted in white in the left corner
CHUCK PETTiS "El chico de la luz".
donde esta la luz down here? i think
people etch it into the wood and then
transfer it onto paper, which is also wood, but
spread so thin and pasty it doesn't remember
chlorophyll.

i want people to see me as human because
where i come from we tell stories about
how humans die after experiencing all
the colors in the world. the brown on
the gray cubicle walls could be coffee.
could be blood that's rusted and faded
but still remembers flowing. i don't
recall trees growing in this shade of brown.

when i travel back to my dimension (either by
force or naturally, a one-way portal) and
the beings ask me what i've learned about
being human, i will tell them i learned
how to sit at a desk with a bent back and
bowed neck to write poetry. i will tell them
how i traced with my left index finger
every tan scar webbing wood that refused
to warp. i will tell them with a sigh that dinosaurs
aren't saints, and humans can't even be sure
what colors they were.

just as the fathers intended

on the 246th birthday of some aging parchment
written by white men declaring autonomy from
some other white men wearing red, i wear red
and orange on my tank top that says rome.
i roam around a man-made lake encircled
by fat worms of duck and geese shit, trapping
heat in my black hair beneath my black
witch hat, trapping virtual monsters grinning
in pixels on my phone. at home i am trapped
with my black cat inside, by the fear of gunshots
that have already transmogrified this nation
into a coagulation of red. i make black
rice noodle miso soup with bok choy
while reading amanda gorman, sianne ngai,
best things to beat the summer heat on buzzfeed.
there are no *happy 4th* texts, just *stay safe* and
keep reading. brown skin darkens in the window
as black words heat through my palms. in the black
of night there are five separate places bursting
with light visible from my balcony, smoke wafting
up the street illuminated by red. at least i am not
trapped by a girlfriend, but i am instead trapped
by a white man in power who says it should not be so.
i look into my albino snake's red eyes and finally
understand. this is what it means to be free.

vocal ransom note from a witch

to whom it may or may not concern—

he-hello–is this thing on? it beeped–
        crashing noises
HIKARI STOP

please, please take hikari back. i tried calling
her parents, but they claimed they didn't
have a daughter. her friends say that

my suffering is earned. when i tried
boiling her in soup, she ate all the
potatoes before i could find the coriander

and salamander's foot. i tried sealing away
her voice in a box, but it leapt out at me
and kept making fun of my warty nose.

the local dragon already kidnapped a local
princess, so he can't take her. the fairies say
she's too big, even though she's tiny

for a human. i thought her magic hair
would have healing powers, but it cut me
like a katana at first touch. she drank

my blood and now i think she may be
part vampire. she put on my flesh-eating hat
and turned it vegetarian. she pet my black cat

and now it follows me around nonstop, asking
for pets and treats. hikari ate all the cat food. i am offering
$1,000 plus five pieces of dragon gold to the entity

that can take her away. please. gods know
i'm so tired. oh no, she found my ancient herbs
and no no no stop eating them please no more

crashing noises continue

to the things i need to stop writing about

to sky—

        let me rip you into tattered ribbons,
        jar your staticky clouds in vinegar.
        my mother would love to eat you
        with her tilapia for dinner tomorrow.

to wind—

        please get out of my mouth.
        you'd be a whole lot more interesting
        if my hair wasn't in knots
        and you didn't smell like flowers.

to clenched fists—

        all of them. haven't you ever heard of
        cuddling, or cupping pink-skinned birds?
        get off of instagram for two hot seconds.
        maybe three. take a walk on the beach at sunset.

to serpents—

        my darlings. my dearest, smooth, sanguine
        lines. you've become expensive and, i hate to say
        constricting. i will always admire your star-struck
        unblinking sky moon eyes. even if you can't see the moon.

to mud—

        you've done it already. been delicious as cake batter.
        dried as bones, graveyard for magicians and tadpoles.
        your lines are still wet and fresh as ~~alligator's~~ tongues, but
        your expiration date is manifest destiny. pack a sandwich and get.

to hearts—

        it ain't valentine's day, and even if it was,
        you don't occupy my apartment rent-free.
        i'm as empty and cold as a dead kid's halloween
        candy bucket. you're just not my type.

to dreams—
        i'll just give you a quick julienne, dress you in pink
        peppercorns. there's a seagull about to land on the pier
        and his breastbone sticks out. his eyes glisten, his beak tip red
        as hearts as murder. you're bold enough to be digested on your own.

self-portrait as a haunted house

/ when was the last
time anyone washed
the bedsheet & who
gets to see the corpse
beneath its egyptian
cotton thread suff-
ocation what
do you mean you
can't ascertain
the attic's location
the bulb still works
the spiders think
it's too clean to
weave anything
not made of lav-
ender soap &
kissed softly with
wildflower honey /

/ not cracked or black
or even ghost gray but
still spooky so everyone
screams banshees when the
foundations start groaning
again & the scent of anti-
dandruff shampoo inhales
itself into the livings'
pink wet mouths like
september into re /

/ member one is a snake
& member two is a snake
& member three is a snake
& oh gosh all the members
are snakes in blue going
through ecdysis in the
barred piano room /

/ no jeans only t-shirt
dresses & long socks
& somewhere a gilded
chest full of hairbows
of every color though
the wood is brown &
borrowed & broken /

/ too many pictures act-
ually gigantic postcards
blue tacked to the walls
commanding pastels to
dance in the ballroom
lacking a chandelier so
instead there's a sliver
of mirror a shard of sun
sky forgot to pack up /

/ something vividly pink
stands in the corner like
a headless mannequin
not smooth headless because
it came that way head-
less because some angry
entity decided to placate
itself by separating foam
from form & neckline from
jaw tossed in the tumble-
weed garden now let's
talk about that monstrosity /

/ statues rock bone plastic
concede to earth & even
the moss is cracked dust
& their ghosts play bridge
on the zen bridge whispering
good vibes only please /

/ you can come in no
one cares about knocking
anymore so just knock the
door in because some kid
from marching band stole
the doorknob as a dare
come in come in come in /

~~Love Letter~~

i said i would never / stretch my words / into rice noodles / wear them like a / hat / then splinter / them like rosewood / a sunken sour / marimba A# /

yet here / they are / though you will / never know you / coiled like / a rope of dust / worn fuzzy / with care / the scent of tortilla chips / permeating twilight / blending into / sleepy pillow musk /

frozen hands / slick with something / natural / which actually means / glycerin-free / sliding slow / as slugs / trailing wet / across the landscape / of your skin so / so like mine and yet / and yet /

the future is / a shut-down circus / striped tent dun / fluttering slow / flattened like a cloud / within someone else's / fortune-telling / palms /

our conversations / chalked like constellations / i wish i could say / they brightened / the night / like vegas / on the first of january / like a birthday candle / before blessed / by breath /

the lovers / drawn reversed / geese flying upside down / rays of light / struck down / and swallowed / as sharp as swords / but minus nightmare / broken by / the gray of dawn /

soothe me again / with your voice / over the phone / over a bowl / of ramen / over the blankets / your breath / a feather / without promise /

movement is expected and / change is not / outrageous / so we can wash / the taste of salt / with zero-calorie vitamin water / and diet cranberry juice / maybe even / boba / burnt brown sugar /

how do i thank you / for not being / rough / for being / enough / for stability of / emotion / for being more / than a face / a name / on a glowing screen / can i just say / i wrote this love letter

one day / i will forget the feel / of your calluses / caused by iron weight / and i will forget / the direction you sweep / your hair / and that day / you will read this poem /

do it for him

for bitch turtle

the exigence of this poem is that bitches exist, specifically bitchy box turtles
who try to kill any other turtle they could sink their beak into.
the clunky rush of turtle head to another calm turtle's neck is enough
to inspire fear worthy of documentation for any reptilian legend.

i love thinking about how turtles have inspired the best in humanity.
we live on a giant turtle's back, and it serenely paddles her way through
the cosmos as we share our french fries or dig graves for faithful dogs.
their wrinkles remind us of their silent wisdom, their ageless luckiness.

everyone calls bitch turtle auntie b. but upon closer examination—
the concavity of her shell, the position of cloaca further down along
her tail—i am sure that auntie b is acutally uncle b. i would tell
the lead keepers, but i don't want to ruin the fun, or be involved

in difficult decisions such as name changing. mine was already enough.
what would he be, then? asshole turtle, for the cloaca is easy to see an inch
outside of the shell. angy turtle, not rad enough for the letter "r", and too
cute to be an entity with that caustic sound. i already feel the acidity

of his gaze as he rushes towards my brown rubber sperry boot, the only mate
suitable for him. if i had one, i'd tie a red balloon to his shell so i would always
know where he's off to next. he'd never tell me why, or why he goes in his water
bowl as soon as i scrub it and fill it with new water, but i'd always do it, for him.

the sun comes out in february—haiku meditations

oh! i want to to touch
everything the light touches.
nothing touches me.

it's way too early
for this blossoming spring time.
no pink right now, please.

carrots and hummus
by wescott plaza fountain.
damp grass sticks to legs.

lake ella blossoms.
so much duck poop. always, poop.
trees bleed into green.

come again, rain, please.
saturday thunder vibrates
cheer onto frogs' backs.

once it's just a bit
over eighty nice degrees,
rattlesnakes come out.

all tea is tasting
like flowers and chaucer's tears.
think—*whan that aprill...*

soon, eggs will appear:
plastic shells on target shelves.
i buy more carrots.

another day with a distant tiger mom

last night my mother texted me, but this time it wasn't
to ask if i've finished all my "studying". *do good on your work
so you will have a better chance of finishing your program.*

i wish my mom believed in my capabilities like the way how
she believes in god. *god is watching*, she tells me, after i told her
i am caught up on all my reading and writing. when i remind

her i am atheist, she tells me that she didn't raise us that way,
despite her never bringing us to church, never praying in thanks
before our mac n cheese or her pinakbet we always thought

smelled like socks dunked in spoiled tea. *you only had 1
university accepted you for master n phd program.* like i really
needed the reminder of the countless number of rejections

i've earned and quietly store, like cicada shells in jars. husks
of dreams that are faintly scented like the san francisco blackberry
honey i used in my nightly tea. if my mom were to see my honey

shelf, jars stacked against the right side of the wall, she'd take out
a ziploc and bag them all, would ask me why i had so many, where
my money came from, how i spend too much at the store. then

the ziploc would go right back against the side of the wall. she'd
shut the cabinet and peer into my trash, examining the bin to ensure
it's clean. i perceived san francisco as a blessing. she perceived it

as a drain. on resources, finances, a four-hour drive one way, another
floor to clean and fridge to scrub. the day she and my father drove me
back to the central valley, i had wanted to stop by pier 39 and say goodbye

to the sea lions. *no time*, they said, as they shoved the ten-gallon snake
tank into the backseat. she asked me if i had room, but even if i didn't,
there would be no action as a result. maybe i sound ungrateful,

which i'm not. i am the drain, because i want to read and write and study what others are reading and writing. the family farm fortune is dwindling. there's a new car in the garage, but my mom says dad hasn't gotten paid

since february. there's so much i don't understand, from the cross in my car to the breath of white ashes that looms over her mother and my father mother. it's just another day. another lonely night, another poem. another dra

the moon missed being in this one

tiny snail dreams dusk but
mistakes it for lettuce so he
munches into an ombre indigo
sky, waves his eyestalks around
like it's his last birthday, asks
sibilant stars to sing him some
sunny songs. he opens his mouth
to partake in the celestial karaoke
& emanates suspended cymbal
hssssooooooooossssssshhhhhh
during the last chorus. he misses
when he was a blue ballpoint pen
riding in an autistic child's purple
backpack, getting gnawed nonstop
and tap tap tapped against scarred
wooden desks until lunchtime. the
next time he dreams sunset, he asks
the suns' rays to transform him into
a ripe cucumber, because the last
one was summer crisp and delicious.

your internet connection is unstable

swirl   of faintly
            pink
lychee hard   candy
smoothly
        erases
            the sharp of green
                              onions   from
tired   taste buds.
                my olfaction
        my gustation

muted.

                chopped   on amazon
prime
choppy   as   the internet blinks
        in   and   out.
        the round   plump of fruit
breathes
                                    through the
            grainy static   of
                heavy lidded   eyes   and crooked
                toothy
        gashes   of mouth.   your internet
            connection

is unstable.   the
white   font
            is bitter   as dandelion
        greens chopped
                        up with   bites of
sound.   i think
memory   is.   imagination.
                but.
        what about   the leftover

soup
            in the fridge?   who
remembers
                        the battle to   boil
on   a   ow stove   top,
                                    flag
of steam   caressing a
                              burnt
palm   like a
mother's kiss?

                              mother.
        click   of spoon
            against   a black
screen.   water trickles on
  the table
                drips in the sink.
                            wet on wet
                        throat.

fuck ur apps

i once saw a commercial where a girl dies in a car crash and her
phone hits the pavement, still ringing. how a virtual life still runs on,
blissfully, without any regard for the lives it connected, protected,
and built—i used to not understand why people were so attached
until i got my own. i was on the 22 filmore bus in san francisco
catching a pikachu when

someone behind me snatched my phone out of my hands,
leapt out the back door, and ran around the corner.
in the span of two seconds, my life was shoved into a black sweatpant
pocket and everything i knew, except whether or not i caught
that pikachu, was gone. i'll never forget when the bus driver
radioed police, only for them to tell him, "have her call herself."

instead of screaming *on what phone?* i got off the stop and used
the free wifi at the corner cafe to facetime my dad on my ipad.
bless facetime. bless the free hot chocolate, never mind
it being a bit too hot, bless my friend using his iphone to try to
track my iphone (to no avail). from then on i used my phone
with two hands whenever i was on the bus, and put it in my

pocket when it wasn't in use. now that i have my own car,
hiding my phone from lurking strangers isn't the problem,
but rather my phone being in sight while driving. even in the
passenger seat, i still have problems with my phone. like yesterday,
when my friend finally grabbed my phone out of my hands after
my game froze for the fourth time that hour.

it felt odd to be put in that vulnerable situation again, not in control
of the little metallic rectangle that connected me to everything
and everyone i was passionate about. when he asked me when was
the last time i cleared my app cache, before i could say um, he was
furiously swiping up at all my open tabs. he said a lot of things.
the only thing i remember

was "FUCK YOUR APPS" before i was able to get my phone back
and reopen my game. as i laughed, i thought. what a neat concept.
to fuck your apps you spent the most time on and they wouldn't
give a fuck back. one day i'll close something forever, maybe not even
know it would be the last time, and not even give a fuck.
even if that app did, i wouldn't know.

forecast of the heart

tonight there is sleeplessness predicted
until about two in the dark (can't call it
morning if there's no aubade). there's a
rare occurrence of poorly-lit slow piano
ballads, fingertips coated by black dust
that can't be rubbed away, though the stain
is permeated by lavender and the other silent
scents of beauty under the kitchen faucet.

the rapid knock on the door from bleary-eyed
neighbors doesn't resound. a beer bottle shatters
the night somewhere on the street below. before,
flesh of a wrist pressed against the refracted rain
of glass would have clouded any desire for
the ceaseless softness of the still-warm bed. now
is the quiet crunch of a tortilla chip from the
mission district, bruno mars lyrics looping

like an ouroboros. once, i would have put my hand
on a blade (not for you). tonight is devoid of blood
because of you. no one jumps in front of a train
for anyone. tonight there is a desire for morning,
not mourning exploding like a grenade. the potential
for hurt is weapon enough to topple civilizations.

at some point, there will be dreams, as expected—
loudly lonely, senseless as the sway of sweetgrass
in a field watched over by gods of sheep and mule.
be prepared to wake up in a film of sweat before
sunrise. whatever can't be predicted will dispense
one by one, star by star evicted from a birdless sky.

two weeks

hey boss. sorry about
the accident. i didn't mean
for the baby gators to get out

and eat the sun. so to save
myself from further
embarrassment, consider

this my two weeks' notice.
i don't know how we can
measure time anymore

without the sun (my bad),
and we probably won't last
two weeks without it anyways.

don't worry about severance
pay. i was never in this for
the money. i'll miss this job.

self-portrait as a marimo moss ball

at some point (figuratively speaking
since i'm round)
i rolled out of the mud onto shore

where a pudgy grasping hand
squeezed and squeezed me
until i thought i wasn't green.

when i saw myself again, i wasn't brown.

i was placed in a little jar with some white rocks
and a thin bleached twig and sold
for $22 plus tax at an elderly japanese lady's bonsai shop.

now i sit on a kitchen counter dreaming
of what steak tastes like, dreaming of a lake
with murky waters and fluttering comets of fish,
dreaming halcyon muddy dreams.

RE: mid-twenties

after all this trash
talk about bojangle's

and one of the worst
drive thru experiences

of my sad chickenless
life (anxiety flashback I:

what sauce do you want
friend: A LARGE PEPSI)

i can finally say i've conquered
all the fried chicken. but

asian fried chicken is still
the best chicken, especially

the korean street style nuggets
eaten with long bamboo toothpicks.

(anxiety flashback II: friend:
do you have a version of chicken

nuggets? *indistinct muttering*
friend: okay we'll have that)

out of all the things i regret
putting in my mouth over two

and a half decades, fried chicken
is the least of my worries. (anxiety

flashback III: me: can you ask her
if we get straws? friend: eventually)

also, asians don't really have biscuits,
so thank you southern biscuits

for making my life in florida
buttery, fluffy, and so so hot

i'm speechless.

self-portrait as soup

if you have to explain your email signature
to important people, like your boss or some
very high-ranked professors and administration,
you'd better have a damn good explanation

for why you're named after a food. and said
food is just specific enough to raise questions
(unlike maybe durian, which sounds like darien,
which is a real name, right) but not so specific

that said administrator is like, ah yes, it's my favorite
tonkotsu with extra corn and two sheets of nori ramen.
i'm still trying to figure out how to cut down a long
monologue involving my gamer tag on pokémon go

into just: it's me, soup.

V.

kyle told me i sound more awesome than owls even though
all of us (kyle, owls, me) would rather sleep through the day,
unless going to costco is involved

is my english english enough?

every time i make soup i always put in too much water [pause. water is the blood of all soup] and when i pour it into the bowl, no matter how big, the soup spills on the table. the soup stain [pause. the napkin can't wipe all of it, no napkin can do that] is a poem. so it makes sense that every time i want to write a poem, i make soup [pause. i consider cereal and milk to be soup.]

i never knew that my body could produce this much amount of snot when i cry [pause. for crying time.] i'd like to bless whomever invented tissues, because tissues are their own soft poems waiting to be punctuated with bodily fluids. there are lots of tears and blood in poems, but what about snot? [pause. could snot also be a soup?]

i don't understand when people want to share the english language with me or frown when i say that english is also my language. odds are, i have probably written much more than them in english, and i have probably read much more than them in english. [pause. soup recipes are in english, as well as cold medicine directions.] there's the same frown when i tell them i'm from

california, as if california exclusively produces blond male lifeguards with perfectly straight teeth. [pause. i think my teeth are straight enough, straight enough to even be a lifeguard.]

so at night before bed sometimes [pause. this could mean 12am. this could mean 1:13am.] snot drips out of my nose and i wonder if my english is english enough even though i am part of the english department [pause. i have the sticker that says very officially, in a circle, department of english]. maybe i am better suited to the department of silence. the department of rocks, where

we don't give rocks names or anything but we just touch them and nod. [pause. it's always thoughtful nodding, not dismissive.] then in silence, i blow my nose and make some nice soup.

it's the sky's fault

hey, is it still important that the child
within me bites her lip at bruising purples
of impending night? hey, is it still
important for me to feel that exhilarating
blush while i glare knives at my opponent
calling me *bitch* for dealing lethal damage
in a children's card game? hey, is it
still important that i take comfort in
the plush rainbow of adorable stuffed
animals strewn across my bed, soft
ears and solid black eyes stitched
tight and spotless, x's as small butts,
toothless smiles reflecting light in these
bizarrely lukewarm dreams of mine?

i'll admit that some days i just write
poems because i didn't write one the day
before, and suddenly the naked trapeze of
adjectives on the page is asking me
for worker's compensation and the right
to unionize. they don't seem to understand
my fears no matter what type of tea i give
them, but they won't follow me on twitter
or accept my challenges for a friendly
duel. so i give them my giant squishy
dragon and some water for their house-
plants. they stop complaining about
fleas in their beds, and my eyes water
as the sky glazes over like a ripe plum.

my macbook no longer recognizes me

a thank-you to my lenovo yoga i9, which always recognizes me

tell me what i've done, the sins
i've committed in popeyes chicken grease.

is it because you're more of a KFC entity?
machine slick as water rejecting the oil

of my flesh for the second time. i am
unrecognizable. am i fat or gristle?

am i, a misplaced comma, a lopsided equal sign
that looks more like the unacceptable synonym

happy face in ン or ツ ? perhaps joy eludes
you, a shadow deeper than the grooves

of my whorled fingerprint. our worlds
are severed, by glass sharper than disgust.

self-portrait of an american as a dirty kitchen

cherry pie crumbs mingle on the stovetop with sourdough
garlic bread. a clorox wipe pushes them down the crack
between the stove and countertop. welcome to crumb land.

when will the american cheese in my fridge grow mold? when will i?
am i less american for hosting new life, green on neon orange?

water molecules move in the microwave until some become steam.
at the sound of a green beep the steam dissipates. dangling
like an herbal omamori, a diet blueberry matcha tea bag is shoved by a stained

silver spoon to the depths of green blue. then honey. oh, honey. squeeze
of plastic for a translucent moon-mass sinking into sweet.
ceramic burns impatient tongue. you should try earl grey,

my client on the screen says. i will someday, i say. is it a big deal
or a small deal if my sink is full of dirty dishes? is it a big deal
or a small deal if i get 100 poetry rejections? is it a big deal

or a small deal if i never try earl grey?
some invisible hand is slowly peeling a disney poster
off the wall. the same hand refuses to let the stained swinging lid

on the not quite white garbage pail rest center.
strawberry stems in the garbage lurk in empty greek yogurt
containers. strawberry leaf in the sink over blocky crystals

of riced cauliflower. how to spell the grease rim around the soaking pan?
the smell starts with a x. the texture a y. as brown liquid trickles
down the drain, the letters are voiceless. the stained cream of bubbles follows.

what i think of when i am drinking taro boba slushies

at the remnants of midday, the soft chill of lavender dreams
permeate my mouth, coat my tongue with the starch of something
that's in. trendy. fabulous. just exotic for us to claim diversity
and culture. who turned purple into powder? flowered their fields
with rough brown hands, tool blades worn smooth as tapioca?
unknown. irrelevant. just add more sugar, and you'll forget.

i chew the shadows of doubt from the depths of cream
slowly, to see if i can taste the stories behind storefronts.
somewhere there are poems. at least one. if i keep drinking,
they'll spill a sanguine slush of words into my stomach. if
they're sonnets, i'll vomit. i form my mouth around those
squishy boiled words and hold them gently as roe on my tongue.

ode to fried rice

grains of someone else's fortune
        heap   in my blue china bowl
                                like unread emails
    huge squishy sale!
        next to   plump pink   of shrimp
we couldn't process your automatic payment…
          just a   raft   amongst
      a cosmic swirl   of egg

so maybe i'm not   asian enough
   to own a wok

      so i let   the microwave echo   like my unfed   cat
        his teeth   snagging
my dog lover socks   while
      steam bites   my careless   fingertips

in the space   in which i wander away to   satiate the   angry
    i wonder   about the unctuousness   of dusk
      wilting
        into   night
             a cut of scallion
             into dark
wet heat—

chopsticks have   outgrown
         the dice of vegetables   slick
             with oil
    or fat
      like the pudge   outgrowing
  my gauchos

it must be   fat
      i use a   spoon
         anyways

loveless sunday

I

enter: piano music playlist
chalk-streaked sky
crooked china blue area rug with cat litter
falling onto scratched wood floor.
swiffer wet mop streaks. chemical lemon zest. zero unread messages.
too old for the clean up song but not "let it go". foam snow white
of a mr. clean sponge soiled by thursday's pork belly grease
exhaled by sizzling fat.
mint green swirl of toilet flush striated with hair long enough
for an entire music score.
end scene.

II

enter: burnt out lightbulb above
fresh black printer ink beneath
men.[1] *do*[2] protecting the base of a lamp.
kote[3] thrown carelessly behind in the corner.
moonstone beams on a black t-shirt dress.
remember, it says in blue undertones,
remember where you've fought, and i don't mean harvard.
kote stand leaning into the corner. they gossip.
the words ancestors and waste get thrown on the unmade bed.
does she even know how to tie her hakama[4] *anymore?*
end scene.

III

enter: one (1) one-hundred and twenty-six (126) page manuscript
       rejected ten (10) times.
x stands for the amount of poems thrown into a folder labeled
       "fantastic nightmares".
y stands for the volume of ink crusting in unused pens.

---

[1] head

[2] side

[3] wrist

[4] type of traditional japanese clothing

z stands for the number of anti-anxiety pills left.
        on youtube, a slime making video plays silently
        in the dark of early evening.
        an enjambment of glitter. the swirl of kennings.
        ice cream smooth syntax.
        lines chime clear as glass. speech bubble pop soundlessly.
        insert loud squelching, sucking noises here.
        it's called an ars poetica.
end scene.

IV

enter: dusty piano. dusty crystals. dusty houseplants.
shinai [5] in the bag asking when the *tsuba* [6] will be taken off.
an email just for rejections, across *t,* which stands for time.
a fluffy plague doctor staring at a jar of oxygenated
blueberry-scented slime.
        "once upon a dream" waltzes across the dining room table.
        i know you. but i don't know what you do.
        chipotle's free delivery isn't enough to satiate a starving tongue.
        one blue pill each night means no depression, but the side effect
        is depression. the swivel chair spins round and round at the desk.
        no one sees.

end scene.

---

[5] bamboo sword used for sparring in kendo
[6] the wrist guard of the shinai

night-soured lullaby

in this decade / i have plastic / retainers / tasting like / curdled cream / under a dreaming / crescent moon / reminding me / i'm still healing /

open mouth / sneezes / onto my thin / comforter / curled ice toes / snagging / a thread / tissue box / tumbling as / i fumble / for a tissue / snot and tears / running into / my hingeless yawns /

muted within / my pillow / sings deep glassiness / of whale song / a notification / a dewdrop / a star / asking me / what about the dark / is frightening / and did you / remember /

to brush / your teeth / and swallow / your medicines / chew / blackberry / melatonin gummies / a ritual / followed / to the last / grain / of hydroxyzine / and did you / remember /

to moisten / your finger / dab away / dried white / toothpaste fleck / on the minty / bathroom / mirror / and did you / remember /

to ask / the dark / hair / on the toilet seat / how it got there / before brushing / it off / then / flushing / it away / and did you / remember /

to wonder / whether you're just / a naïve / unprofessional / loud / arm flapper / or whether / you should actually / see a spectrum / specialist /

the taped notices / e-mails / marijuana smoke / wafts / like waifs / invisible / wail / fainter / as time / pares itself / down to / a skeleton / clean air / a myth / underneath / the bed /

as i suck / green scent / into my lungs / and whale song / dies to / a throaty / hum / hair / whispers its way / into my / melatonin mouth / asking / when i'll be good / enough /

in another decade / i put my hands / around the infant face / of morning / roll it into play-doh / noodles / tie it behind my back / an illuminated / apron /

my soul as an ita-bag

ouch! when will you be done
poking my yellow belly full
of holes? please make up
your mind. i'm getting heavy.

do i absolutely adore displaying
a window into myself, ripe with
shiny treasures? as long as no one
sees the back, it's fine, right?

center: white cat playing violin-baguette.
left: ミルク carton with cow-dressed corgi.
top: boba-saur and guinea pig in an orange.
bottom: sad tempura, stranger than fiction.

right: the sailor of destruction, but cute.
look at me! i'm cute, dark, full of food
i can never digest. if you close your eyes,
you can hear me hanging happy from your door.

meteorite queso

somehow i figured out there was a meteorite shower
between the hours of midnight and 5:30am, but being

slightly sick and with no chance of being awake, i shrugged
it off and hoped nothing would crash through my roof.

at 11:11, i was alerted it was 11:11 over facetime.
make a wish, i said, and my twin brother says, *hm*.

i say, i wish that a meteorite lands on my balcony, and
it's filled with queso. he tells me that would be so

good, as long as the cheese hadn't dried out.
i think about all the white queso oozing onto my balcony,

and am slightly disgusted by the thought of crunchy
cheese. and then i realized–i have no chips.

introducing my girl band, wet sidewalk

we drink mogu mogu with extra nata de coco
out of mushroom cups, headbang until our air-
pods clatter onto the scratched laminate floor.

we sing songs about why the sidewalk is wet.
our playlist: someone dropped their coconut sorbet.
someone told me a lie and now the sky is falling
out of my eyes. a frog hopped across searching
for some other frog to amplexus. someone spit.
my brother threw a snowball and missed. we miss
our deceased dog. the hose is leaking. the clouds
wouldn't stop pouting. ballpoint pen explosion.

we cry if we drop our miki noodle soup. we cry
because the snakeskin ripped and now the cat
is pawing it around. we cry because children
are full of bullets instead of pichi-pichi or
malasadas. we cry for the lifespan of dragonflies.

we collaborate, too. featuring: the sound of the newest
iphone dropping onto our ex-partner's driveway. the wind
(wednesday afternoon without trees). my pregnant
mother angrily shouting for dinuguan, circa 1996.
a wishbone breaking unevenly. the microwave screaming
to the world that leftover pancit is ready. breaking mirror.

we are unapologetic. we don't shave, we don't slave
for nobody. unless, now, hear us good and clear:
there is free, all you can eat halo-halo. with extra ube.

stop telling me to be stronger

it's 4am yet my dreams dance
so dust doesn't settle on them. i don't shed
a tear when the dancing stops and words begin:
i'm not necessary. i'm fooling myself.
i only cringe a little when i read about red alarm bells
going off in a girl's head when his hands start moving
down her body. *my body isn't his. my body isn't*
anyone's. i can meet him or her or them
make steak and love, bake bread and break bonds
and believe it's not my fault. fault is fragile.
like night it shatters at the whisper of light.
i don't need to wrap myself in weighted blankets
or cheesy tortillas or even clear-broth-clear-conscious soup
when i think of the possibility of love, even one
that loses effervescence after sitting stale in a fridge.
i can grasp a future without pills and high bridges
over hard water. i can cut through apples, leave clean
knives in the drawer without shrinking from their fierceness.
it's 4am and at the sound of another car alarm,
i waltz into the blush of dawn in c major.

one poem closer

to the cracked black peppercorn silence
of the cast iron universe. one swirl more
of honey dissolving into chamomile tea
as i roll unbaked gingerbread dough

across the powdered field of flour.
long ago, beings with light in their hair
and wings and talons told us how
they stole the night egg from the great

sky dragon, cracked the shell to release
the yolk moon, and rolled it across
the milky way. my dough is still
too wet. a handful of flour more.

an empty plastic bag decades from
becoming dust. how many blades
will it ribbon through, how many
flames before it can glow soft

with the ghostliness of moonlight?
one poem closer to the shifting
of the heavens, one hand of flour
closer to the scent of cloves and

comfort. for the first time this season,
a book page turns with all the delicacy
of a phoenix wingbeat. one sonnet closer.
closer still to the hum of the oven, or the stars.

acknowledgments

big thanks to my Pokémon GO community, my biological and non-biological families, social media followers, literary magazines, University of San Francisco MFA cohort, Florida State University cohort, coworkers, and friends. i'd like to thank the team at Cornerstone Press, particularly Dr. Ross K. Tangedal, Grace Dahl, Sophie McPherson, Natalie Reiter, and Ava Willett, for their patience and professionalism as we worked to get my first book out into the literary world.

---

some of my poems have appeared (in various stages in development) in the following literary magazines:

Aurora Journal
Brave Voices Magazine
Broadkill Review
Chestnut Review
Cobra Milk Magazine
Eunoia Review
Fleas on the Dog
Haunted Waters Press
Honey Literary Magazine
Horse Egg Literary
Justice For All
Litbreak
MacGuffin
Moss Puppy Magazine
Peatsmoke Journal
Red Wheelbarrow
The Wondrous Real Lit

Hikari Leilani Miya is an LGBTQ Japanese-Filipina American who graduated from Cornell University in 2019 with a BA in English, and from the University of San Francisco with an MFA in Creative Writing. She is a doctoral student in Florida State University's program in creative writing, and she holds a Master's Certification in herpetology from the Amphibian Foundation. Her poems have been published or are forthcoming in dozens of in-print and online magazines across North America, including *MacGuffin, Chestnut Review, Eunoia Review, Broadkill Review,* and *Brave Voices.* In 2021, she was a semi-finalist for the Red Wheelbarrow poetry prize judged by Mark Doty.

She currently lives in Tallahassee with her snakes, leopard gecko, and disabled cat, and volunteers at the Tallahassee Museum specializing in reptile care and handling. In addition to earning her master's certification in herpetology from the Amphibian Foundation and certification in husbandry and captive management, she is a former health care worker, percussionist, pianist, and competitive card game player.